Publish That Book Now

Julia A. Royston

Edited by: Kaylee Overbey

B|**K**
ROYSTON
Publishing

BK Royston Publishing

P. O. Box 4321

Jeffersonville, IN 47131

502-802-5385

http://www.bkroystonpublishing.com

bkroystonpublishing@gmail.com

Cover Design: Vikiana

ISBN-13: 978-0692528075
ISBN-10: 0692528075

Printed in the United States of America

Dedication

I dedicate this book to anyone who has ever dreamed of writing a book, wanted to write a book or is currently writing a book. This book is for you!

Acknowledgement

First, I acknowledge my Lord and Savior Jesus Christ for giving me all of my gifts and especially my gift to write His words.

My husband who is always supportive, loving and encouraging me to utilize all of my gifts and talents. Thank you honey.

To my mother, Dr. Daisy Foree, who is my number one cheerleader and always tells me, "hang in there, you can do it." To my father, Dr. Jack Foree, who is never far away from me in my spirit or heart. I only have to look in the mirror each day to see him.

To Rev. Claude and Mrs. Lillie Royston who support me in everything I do.

To the rest of my family, I love you and thank you for your prayers, support and love.

To my great friend Vanessa Collins who told me to write this book years ago. Thanks for being there with me every step of the way. Love you.

Julia Royston

Table of Contents

Introduction

Publish that Book Now is designed to help those who have decided to publish their book on their own. I must caution you that self-publishing is just that, you are doing the publishing yourself. You must write the book, have the book edited, get a cover, format the book, upload to a printing service, secure a way for people to send payments for your book and obtain distribution for your book. A traditional or vanity press provides that service for you. I will discuss the differences between traditional, vanity and self-publishing services.

In the meantime, this book covers the basics of publishing a book yourself. I must give a disclaimer with the contents of this book. Technology changes swift, companies close or consolidate every day, and things printed in this book are subject to change. For the latest updates, conduct your own research and/or reach out to the staff of BK Royston Publishing at www.bkroystonpublishing.com or bkroystonpublishing@gmail.com or call 502-802-5385 for more information.

For information regarding the Write. Publish. Promote Series from Julia Royston, visit: Http://www.writepublishpromoteitnow.com

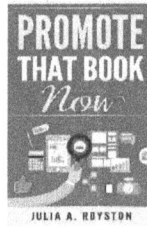

If while during any part of this process you get stuck or need help, feel free to reach out to us at the mentioned website, email or phone number. We provide individualized publishing and writing coaching services.

Let the Publishing Begin!

Traditional vs. Vanity vs. Self-Publishing

A traditional publishing company is just that, the traditional way that books are published. First, an extensive book publishing proposal is submitted to a publishing house through a literary agent and the proposal is either accepted or rejected. The literary agent is paid a hefty fee to shop or propose a book to publishing companies around the country. If the book proposal is accepted, a traditional publisher will give the author an advance check for projected sales of the book as well as handle the rest of the publishing process for the book. The author will retain no rights to their work and will be unable to publish this same work under any other publishing company or themselves. The author will in some cases, not be consulted about the cover design, interior design or distribution outlet of the book in exchange for the story. The publishing company handles all marketing, promotion and distribution of the book. The author will not receive any royalties until after the publishing has made their money back. After the publishing had recouped all costs then the author will receive the minimum amount of royalties for each book that is sold.

A Vanity publishing company is a publishing company that provides publishing services but the author has to pay for all aspects of the book publishing process. However, the author also retains all rights to his or her book and is consulted throughout the publishing process. The author also receives quarterly royalties based on the online sales of his or her book. The author will have to pay for the book to be printed but retains all of the profits from the physical sales of the book. The vanity publishing company usually provides editing, graphic cover design, formatting, printing and distribution of the book for a fee. Some vanity publishing companies do provide marketing, promotion and book launching services but this is also for an additional fee.

Self-Publishing is just that, an author publishes the book themselves. The author is responsible for finding a person to do the editing, and formatting of the book as well as finding someone to print and upload the book to distribution companies. The author will also have to make sure that they have set up a way to receive royalties.

As an author, you have a decision to make when it comes to how you wish to publish your book. There are several publishing companies out there in the world. Do your homework and make the decision that you feel is right for you. Make sure that you read the contract thoroughly and ask as many questions as you feel comfortable with. Seek out a lawyer to review the contract and help you make the right decision. Consider asking other published authors for advice. There are hundreds of them on social media that would be happy to offer advice about how they published their book. Visit http://www.bkroystonpublishing.com and reach out to any of the authors on that website to ask them about their experiences. Make the decision of which publishing path you will pursue and stick to it.

For the purposes of this book, we will be exploring the methods and processes to publish your own book without the need for a publishing company. Yes, I am about to give away my publishing secrets and strategies! I will also be using pictures from my published books to give you a visual of what the parts of the book should look like.

There will also be a video series available to accompany this book. It will walk you step by step through the publishing process. Visit www.writepublishpromoteitnow.com. Remember, you can do this all by yourself but if you get stuck then don't hesitate to reach out to www.bkroystonpublishing.com or www.juliaroystonenterprises.com for assistance and help with going through the processes of formatting, printing and distributing your book yourself.

Let's get your book published!

Editing the Manuscript

The first step in the publishing process is to make sure that you have a professionally edited book. There are plenty of editing services out there but each company charges differently for their service. Some companies charge by the word, line, or page. Know exactly what the charge is for the editing prior to paying for the process. Also, it is important to know what type of editing you are receiving. Is it grammatical editing only? Grammatical editing is editing for just that, grammar. For example, are the words spelled correctly, do the subjects and verbs match and is there correct punctuation for each sentence?

There are content editors who only review your manuscript for the contents or text. These editors offer suggestions on how you could write a better manuscript which would include character and plot development for fiction books or ways to make your manuscript more clear for the reader if it is a non-fiction or self-help book.

If you contracted and paid for grammatical editing, don't expect content editing to be included. Some editors are thorough and offer suggestions anyway, but this is not always the case. On the other hand, if you paid for content editing, don't expect your grammar to be changed or for changes to be suggested. You get what you pay for. It will cost more if you would like grammar and content editing but how important is your manuscript to you? That will determine what you request and pay for. If you are publishing the book yourself, you will have to find a professional editor or request the services of a good, retired English teacher who was hard on you in school but also thorough.

Normally, editing takes between 1-3 weeks to complete depending on the size of the book, the content of the manuscript submitted, and the editor's schedule.

When the manuscript is returned from the editor, make the suggested changes quickly. The sooner that you revise and make corrections to your manuscript, the sooner that you will be able to move forward in the publishing process. You don't necessarily have to agree with the editor, but if grammar is your weakness then you should follow the advice of a trained professional.

Once you have made the corrections, put the book away for at least a week and then pick it up and read it from cover to cover. Read the book out loud because your eyes and head will fool you but your ears will let you know when something doesn't make sense, or doesn't sound right. This will help you catch the last few editing mistakes or things that were overlooked in the editing process. Professional editors are great, but they're still human.

If you don't trust your own eyes and ears, let someone else read an electronic version of your book. This will allow another person to read the book and determine if they agree with the flow of your content. The book made sense in your head when you wrote it but does it make sense to someone else who is reading it? Write the vision and make it plain so that others who read it will understand it. It is imperative that you have another pair of eyes read and review your book before you publish it to the world. The world paid for your book so, they should not find any errors, confusion or layout issues with your book. You owe it to your readership to provide an excellent product.

Order of Pages for the Book

There is a standard order of pages and content that the reader will be looking for when they open your book. This is called the format or layout of the book. Below you will find the correct order of the pages that should be included in your book. If you don't have the pages in this order then you will have to develop those pages and put them in the correct order.

The Front Pages of the book

The front pages of the book are the pages in the beginning of the book directly after the cover. I encourage you to browse through published books to get an idea of what you like and what you want your book to look like once it is published.

The front pages include the title page, copyright page, dedication, acknowledgement, foreword (if desired), table of contents as well as an introduction of the book. Below is the order of the front pages for a standard book.

The Title Page

The title page is just that, the title of your book. The title page should include the title of the book, your name as the author, the editor's name and the illustrator's name and if you establish as a publishing company, the name, city and state of your publishing company.

Title of the book: Begin Again

Author: Julia A. Royston

Edited by: Claude R. Royston

Publisher information:

BK Royston Publishing

Jeffersonville, IN

Begin Again

Julia A. Royston

Edited by: Claude R. Royston

BK Royston Publishing
Jeffersonville, IN

----------- Page Break -----------

11

Copyright Page

The copyright page is your ownership or disclaimer page. The copyright page is the very next page after the title page of the book. The copyright page should include the name of your publishing company, if you have one, the mailing address and contact information including your email and website.

The copyright date of the book which should be the year that the book is copyrighted by the copyright office. We will talk about copyright later but the year that your book will be published should be included here.

The disclaimer states that no parts of the book can be used without the author's permission. The ISBN number, which we will talk about later. The LCCN number, which will be discussed further, and the graphic designer of the cover can be listed here as well as where the book was printed.

BK Royston Publishing

P. O. Box 4321

Jeffersonville, IN 47131

502-802-5385

http://www.bkroystonpublishing.com

bkroystonpublishing@gmail.com

Cover Design: Bill Lacy

ISBN-13: 978-0692666043

Printed in the United States of America

---------------------- Page Break ----------------------

Dedication Page

The dedication page is the page where you can dedicate your book. Some authors dedicate their books to family members, or people who the book is about. An example of this would be, "I dedicate this book to all of those who are caregivers to people with the Alzheimer's disease." The dedication page is usually not very long. It is optional and not a requirement but it can important to the author to give special recognition and dedication of their book to a person, place or thing that is significant to the development of the book.

Below is a sample dedication page:

I dedicate this book to anyone who has ever had something happen in your life that made you start all over again. Know that you may be delayed but destiny still is front of you and you will get there. God's promises are true and absolute.

Dedication¶

¶

I dedicate this book to anyone who has ever had something happen in your life that made you start all over again. Know that you may be delayed but destiny still is front of you and you will get there. God's promises are true and absolute. ¶

Just Begin Again... ——————Page Break——————¶

Acknowledgement Page

The acknowledgement page is designed to give credit or thanks to anyone related to the production of the book. Acknowledge the inspiration behind the book, editor, publisher, family, friends or anyone related to the book.

Example of an acknowledgement,

First, I acknowledge my Lord and Savior Jesus Christ for giving me all of my gifts and especially my gift to write His words.

My husband who is always supportive, loving and encouraging me to utilize all of my gifts and talents. Thank you honey.

To my mother, Dr. Daisy Foree, who is my number cheerleader and always tells me, "hang in there, you can do it." To my father, Dr. Jack Foree, who is never far away from me in my spirit and in my heart. I only have to look in the mirror each day to see him.

To Rev. Claude and Mrs. Lillie Royston who support me in everything I do. Especially, Rev. Royston for his careful eye to detail and his sensitive heart to content.

To the rest of my family, I love you and thank you for your prayers, support and love.

Acknowledgements¶

¶

First, I acknowledge my Lord and Savior Jesus Christ for giving me all of my gifts and especially my gift to write His words. ¶

My husband who is always supportive, loving and encouraging me to utilize all of my gifts and talents. Thank you honey. ¶

To my mother, Dr. Daisy Foree, who is my number cheerleader and always tells me, "hang in there, you can do it." To my father, Dr. Jack Foree, who is never far away from me in spirit and in my heart. I only have to look in the mirror each day to see him. ¶

To Rev. Claude and Mrs. Lillie Royston who support me in everything I do. Especially, Rev. Royston for his careful eye to detail and his sensitive heart to content.¶

To the rest of my family, I love you and thank you for your prayers, support and love. ¶

¶

------Page Break------¶

Table of Contents

The next portion of the book should be the table of contents. All books do not require a table of contents. A table of contents is not necessary in a 30 day devotional because you normally open the book and after the front pages then the book starts with day one and continues. If the book has been divided into chapters then there should be a table of contents. The table of contents should include where the dedication and acknowledgement pages begin as well as the page numbers for each chapter.

Table·of·Contents¶

¶

Introduction

The introduction of the book introduces the book to its readers. The introduction is not the book itself but just introduces the book's background, why you wrote it, gives some basic truths behind the premise of the book and prepares the reader for the manuscript. There is no standard page length for the introduction but if the introduction is not enticing to the reader then why would they turn to page one and begin reading it? The introduction should help make the reader excited to turn to page one and begin reading the book.

Go to the public library or a local bookstore and browse through the topics and genre of books that you are publishing. Open a few books to get examples of what the front pages should look like. Check the font styles and sizes to get an idea of what you like about the look of the text. Do not recreate the wheel if you don't have to. If you don't recognize the font right away then take a quick picture of the text and compare it with the word processing fonts that you have at home on your computer.

You are in the business of publishing your own book so, you should be a student of books and what they look like. The formatting, styles and fonts included in books are as varied as their titles. There are literally millions of books in the world and there are that many variations of how the book is formatted.

_____

_____

_____

_____

_____

_____

_____

_____

_____

_____

_____

_____

_____

_____

_____

_____

_____

_____

_____

_____

The Body of the Book

Now that you know what the front pages are for in your book, it is time to format the meat or heart of your manuscript that comes immediately after the introduction if you have included one.

Layout and Formatting

Your manuscript should be typed and edited by using a word processing software or online editing website such as Microsoft word, Microsoft Publisher, Google Drive, One Drive Word or another Open Word Processing software.

The next phase in the publishing process is the formatting phase. What size do you want your book to be? Go to the library or bookstore with a ruler and decide. After publishing several books, you will know on sight what size the book is by placing it in your hands. Standard printing sizes should be included on the printer's website. For the majority of books, the size is 6 x 9, 5.5 x 8.5 or 8.5 x 11. The first number is the width of the book and the second number is the height of the book.

Open your manuscript in the word processing software that you are using. If using Microsoft Word, open the document. Go to Layout and click on size. This will give you the option to change the page size of the book. The default size of a document is 8.5 x 11, change the width to 6 inches and the height of the book to 9 inches and make sure that you keep the margin of 1 inch all of the way around the manuscript. You will need an inch margin for the printing process. The printer must have an inch margin all of the way around the text so that when the book is put together, the words are not cut off by the spine.

You will notice that you will have a sudden increase in the number of pages of the book. The amount of pages in a manuscript will usually become one and half to double the amount of pages. If you have a manuscript that is currently 50 pages, after you have changed the size of the document, you may have 80-100 pages depending on the amount of text and the spacing within the manuscript. If the book is double spaced, it will almost immediately double in the number of pages.

Begin each new chapter on the right hand side of the page. When you open a book, chapter one should begin on your right after the front pages of the book are complete. Depending on the number of front pages, you may have to insert an extra page so that chapter one begins on the right hand side of the page. The pattern of beginning a chapter on the right hand side of the page should be consistent throughout the book. The right side of the page should be page numbered as an odd number. When you turn the page, the back side of that first page should be numbered an even number. The first page should be page one and the backside of that page should be numbered page two and so on.

Each page is a side of the paper not the number of pieces of paper that are +- included in the book. So, each piece of paper in the book will be the equivalent of two pages. For example, one piece of paper in the book should be numbered as one on the front and two on the back. The next piece of paper in the book should be numbered as three on the front and four on the back and so on. Don't worry, you will get the hang of it. It was confusing to me at first as well. The amount of pages in the book is not the number of pieces of paper but, the amount of front and back pages that contain text and/or images in the book.

Determine your font

The size of your font will determine how many pages that your book will have. If your book is a size sixteen font then there will be more pages. Think back to when you were typing papers in school and you had to have at least ten pages. Mysteriously, the font size got bigger and bigger because this creates more pages. I, personally prefer a size fourteen font. It is large enough but also small enough. You are the publisher now so, make that decision on your own. If the font size is big enough for your grandmother to read it then it is probably the right size.

The style of the font will also make a difference as to how easily your words are read. Compare fonts of the same size but different styles and see if there is not a difference because I guarantee that there is a definite difference.

Once you have determined the font size and style, review your book for any spacing corrections. Do you want the entire book to be double spaced or single spaced? Would you like a double space after the headings or subheadings? Again, I suggest that you look at the layout and formatting of different books to determine what looks the best to you. I have formatted books in single space, double space as well as one and half space. As you format more books, you will be able to determine a formatting style based on sight alone. Remember, if you need help just reach out to BK Royston Publishing at www.bkroystonpublishing.com for advice.

Headers and Footers

Over the years, I have come to develop works around their headers and footers. First, I will have a completely separate document for the front pages and then I will have another document for the main content or body of the book. This allows me to have different headers and footers in the front pages of the book to be different from those in the body of the book. There is a way to do this with an entire document, but I am sticking with my work around. If you are more technology savvy than I am then try going for the other approach.

In the front pages document, I do not apply headers but I do insert a footer in the front pages beginning with the copyright page. I format the page numbers as i, ii, iii, etc.

For the body of the manuscript, insert the author's name in the left header, the title of the book in the right header and the page numbers in the footer. The format for the page numbers in the footer should begin with 1, 2, 3, etc. Select whatever font type and size that you desire, but stay away from script if at all possible.

Below is an example of what the front pages should look like.

Begin·Again¶

¶

¶

¶

Julia·A.·Royston¶

¶
¶
¶
¶

Edited·by:··Claude·R.·Royston¶

¶
¶
¶

BK·Royston·Publishing¶
Jeffersonville,·IN¶

······························Page Break ·····························¶

Julia A. Royston

BK Royston Publishing
P. O. Box 4321
Jeffersonville, IN 47131
502-802-5385
http://www.bkroystonpublishing.com
bkroystonpublishing@gmail.com

Cover Design: Bill Lacy

ISBN-13: 978-0692666043

Printed in the United States of America

---Page Break---

The body of the manuscript should look like this with headers and footers included.

|Action· Plan¶

¶
Vision·Board·Parties,·Meetings,· Luncheons·and·workshops·have· recently·been·all·the·rage·especially·at· the·beginning·of·a·new·year.··I·think·that· all·of·these·events·are·great,·but·having· a·vision·and·putting·that·vision·into· action·are·two·different·things.··I·have· seen·vision·boards·collect·dust·and· nothing·on·the·board·come·to·fruition.·· More·than·a·vision·board·or·vision·plans· or·vision·goals·you·need·to·have·an· action·plan.··What·are·you·going·to·do·to· make·your·vision·come·to·pass?··When· are·you·going·to·have·that·action·step· done·and·completed?··Set·a·date.··Even· if·it·is·not·exact,·set·a·target·date.·When· you·have·something·that·you·are· shooting·for·or·aiming·at,·there·is· motivation,·drive·and·a·great·chance·for· effort·to·be·put·forth·to·make·that·goal· come·true.··¶

---------------------------------Page Break---------------------¶

1¶

¶

Julia·Royston¶

For more information on creating the headers and footers, see the complete video step by step series that will accompany this book. I spent years trying, making errors, correcting mistakes and learning how to make books look great on the inside. There is always something new to learn but I really love the book layouts that I have created so far and you can do it too.

_____

_____

_____

_____

_____

_____

_____

_____

_____

_____

_____

_____

_____

_____

_____

_____

_____

_____

_____

_____

About the Author Section

After the body of the book has been completed, an extended biographical sketch of the author with additional contact information will be included in an 'about the author' section.

The 'About the Author' section is at the very end of the book before the back cover. If you have a book that includes a biography and source page then the 'About the Author' section will begin after these pages.

Here is a sample of the "About the Author" section of a book.

About· the· Author¶

¶
Julia Royston is an author, publishing ·
and motivational speaker born and ·
raised in Louisville, KY. ··Julia is the ·
oldest of 3 daughters in a Christian ·
family and is married to Mr. Brian K. ·
Royston. ··Julia earned a B.A. in ·
Accounting, two Masters Degrees in ·
Information Science and a doctorate in ·
Religious Education from Bellarmine ·
University, University of Kentucky, ·
Spalding University and Grace Bible ·
College, Niles, OH, respectively. ·Julia ·
is a public elementary school ·
Computer Technology Teacher/Media ·
Specialist by profession.¶
¶
Julia has appeared on The Bobby Jones ·
Presents New Artist Showcase and ·
ministered with notables such as Dr. ·
Jackie McCullough, Pastor Donnie ·
McClurkin, Bishop Noel Jones, Bishop ·

57¶
¶

38

Codes of Distinction

Once you have formatted your book, there is some additional information that needs to be obtained prior to uploading the finished document to the printer.

ISBN

You will need an ISBN number associated with your book. ISBN stands for the International Standard Book Number. An ISBN number is a unique number that is attached to a particular title, author and format of a book. Every book should have a unique ISBN number to distinguish it from any other book. You should have an ISBN for the book in paperback, and hardback. You should even have an eISBN number for ebooks. To purchase ISBN numbers, visit www.bowker.com. Bookstores will not sell your book in their store without an ISBN number. Your book should have an ISBN whether you purchase it from Bowker.com or obtain it for free from a self-publishing site, such as www.createspace.com.

The ISBN number should go on the copyright page on the inside of the book and on any promotional materials regarding the book. The ISBN can be searched for online and if your book has global distribution then people can purchase it from their local bookstore for their personal use.

Barcode

The barcode on a book is similar to a barcode on any other product. It allows for the book to be scanned by a barcode reader which allows for the purchase of the book. As a standard, the barcode goes on the bottom right hand corner on the back cover of the outside of the book. The barcode can also be included on promotional materials regarding your book as well. Barcodes can be purchased from www.bowker.com.

Cover of the Book

I cannot tell you how important the cover of a book is to its success. I often go back and forth when it comes to deciding between whether the outside or the inside of the book is the most important. They are both very important but the inside of the book will rarely be seen if the outside of the book is not appealing, and does not clearly represent the inside of the book and its message.

A book may be a number one bestseller but if the cover is not appealing then people won't buy it. That is often the reason why when authors change the book cover, the book starts to sell. The author may not have changed one single word on the inside but when the cover changed, the sells changed. I am a living witness to this fact and I am transparent enough to show you what changing a cover can do for a book.

The first book cover is to a book titled, "Everyday Miracles" which is an

inspirational, and motivational book of
mine.

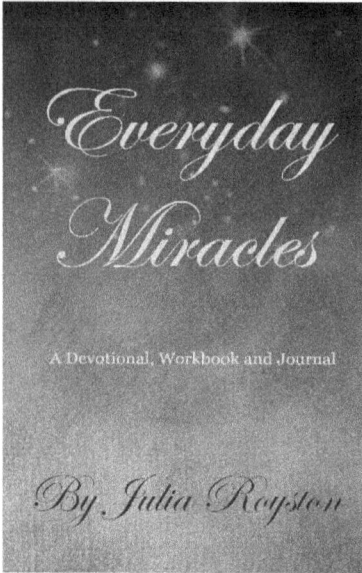

The first cover is not too bad and it did
appeal to some people and I sold some
books. I even did the cover myself. Not
bad, but when I made the sacrifice and paid
a professional graphic artist then I saw a big
difference. Look at what he came with for
the new cover of the book.

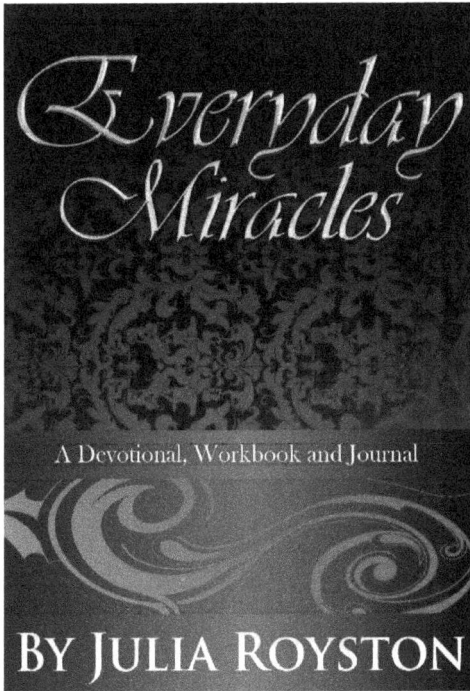

The difference between the first cover and the second is as different as night and day. The colors for the second cover are vibrant. The font is clear and people can see the cover from across the room. Now, if a reader is not interested in motivational or inspirational materials and writings then it won't matter what type of cover you have on it. On the other hand, if they are a Christian education Director or small group bible study leader then this book sells every time.

Make sure that you have a quality cover. Don't go cheap on the cover. Don't go cheap period but especially not on the cover.

Spine of the Book

The size of the book and number of pages will determine how big the spine of the book will be. My book, Jillian is more than two hundred pages because it is romance fiction and this is typically a longer genre. Thus, the spine of the book is much wider than that of a smaller book with less than one hundred pages.

To determine true dimensions of a book, I use a book cover layout guide that is provided to me by several printers that I use to publish my books. See a sample of what the printer guide looks like below:

If you look closely at the above image, the blue area is where the book cover will actually be cut and your cover must extend through that blue area. The pink areas are essentially the folding areas. The front of the book should be to the right and the back of the book will be in the panel to the left. The spine of the book is in the middle just like your spine is in the middle of your back. There is a sample barcode on the bottom to help you make sure that your description doesn't cover this area. If you follow this outline correctly, you will have a document with a book cover that looks like the following.

I use Microsoft Publisher to create all of my book covers and it works well for me. If you have another software or website that works then use it.

Descriptive Teaser about Your Book

The back of your book will also include promotional materials, online distribution websites, your website and links to your social media postings. You will also need a short descriptive teaser about your book that will entice others to buy it.

If the book is fiction then the description should give little hints about the character, setting and conflict.

If the book is self-help then tell who needs to read the book and what problem it solves.

You will use this short description over and over again throughout many opportunities. Media outlets such as magazines, radio, and television will all want a one sheet or speaker's sheet about the book and that short description should be included with this.

An example of a book descriptive teaser is:

Jillian watched so many of her friends date, get engaged and marry before her. She wondered what was taking so long. Jillian had done all of the right things. She had gone to school, built a thriving company, owned a home, drove a luxury car and dedicated years of service to her church and community. But, where was her love?

Come experience the lessons, longing and love of Jillian Forrester. Have faith, your love is on the way too.

Here is the cover to that same book:

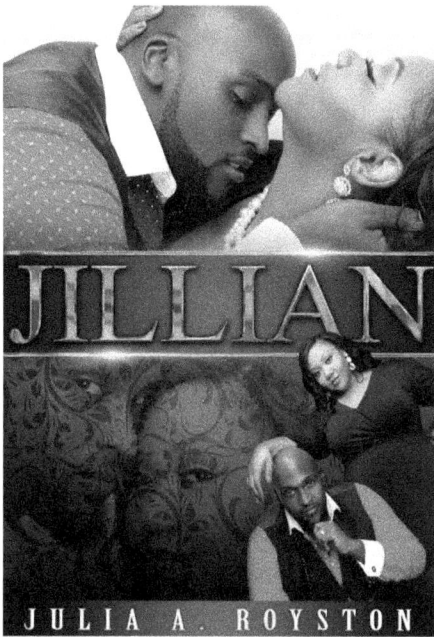

After seeing the cover and reading the description, audiences should be enticed to read your book. That's the point. When the cover and description match it encourages readers to buy the book and make sure that the contents matches as well.

Short Bio of the Author

Earlier, there was mention of an 'About the Author' section which will include a full or extended bio about the author.

For the back cover of the book, you need an abbreviated version of the "About the Author" bio. This short bio about the author can be used in multiple situations including the back cover of the book, a one sheet overview, websites and social media outlets. It is very useful to produce this shortened bio because organizations can use it to introduce you to audiences when you speak.

An example of a shortened bio is below:

Julia Royston is an author, publisher, speaker, teacher and songwriter residing in Southern Indiana with her husband, Brian K. Royston. To her credit, Julia has written original music for 5 Music CDs, 2 DVDs, authored 25 Books, a contributing author in 3 books. Julia and her husband oversee the operation of BK Royston Publishing, LLC to provide quality, informative, inspirational and entertaining materials in the global market place in all media formats.

The non-profit, For the Kingdom Ministries is established to encourage, enlighten and empower people to live the abundant life God promised. By profession, Julia is a certified technology teacher with the local public school system. For more information visit www.bkroystonpublishing.com, www.juliaroystonenterprises.com or www.juliaroyston.net.

Below is a copy of what a finished front cover, spine and back cover will look like when they are ready for the printer. This image shows the book's teaser and description, shortened author bio, QR Code and publishing company logo. The barcode will be added by the printer based on the contract.

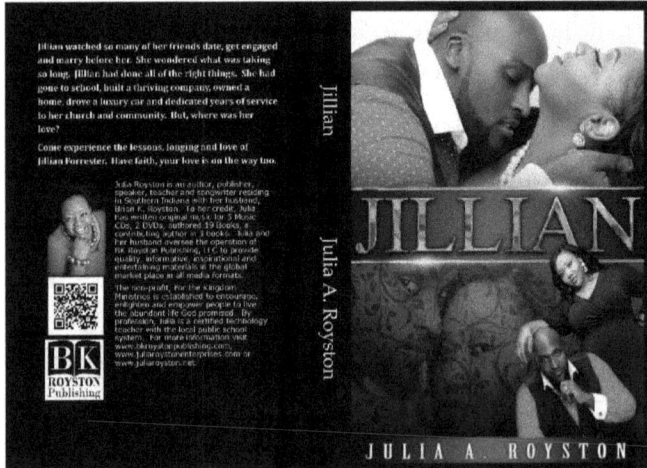

Copyright of the Book

The copyright of the book is the last phase of publishing that I complete before submitting to the printer and obtaining a proof copy of the book.

Visit www.copyright.gov for all of the information that you will need in regards to obtaining copyright ownership of your book. You need to protect the intellectual property or your book. Do not rely on the "poor man's copyright" to protect your book. Fill out the forms, pay the fee and receive your final certificate for copyright ownership of your book. I will not print the exact fee here because it is subject to change but go to www.copyright.gov for all of the latest information on the copyright process for your book.

Your receipt for payment of the copyright fee is your initial proof of ownership. Keep that safe until your final certificate arrives. Receipt of the final certificate from the U. S. Copyright Office takes anywhere from six to eighteen months to complete. Be patient, and consider that billions of items are submitted for copyright approval. When the final certificate arrives it will be well worth it.

A Publishing Company or Personal Publishing

You need to determine if you want to establish a publishing company or publish your book under your personal name. To establish a publishing company, you will need to go through the "Start a Business" procedures with your particular state's Secretary of State or state Business office. This information can be found on your state government's website. I did all of the procedures for my state myself without an attorney but that is left up to you. An attorney or a government entity can advise you on how you should establish your company, as well as its name, classification and the future legal responsibilities.

If you establish a publishing company, you are now officially in business with all of the rights, responsibilities and liabilities associated with owning and operating a business, no matter what the classification.

If you just publish under your personal name and do not establish an actual publishing company then you will still have the responsibilities of doing business but it will directly be associated with your personal assets and property. Do your homework and choose wisely when it comes to how you will publish your book on your own.

Seek legal advice from a professional to protect you, your property and your family.

Method for Royalties and Sales

You need a way to receive money, make payments and record your sales to the Internal Revenue Service. Whether you decide to start your own publishing company or have personal ownership of your book's sales, when you begin to make money, you are in business. You have the same reporting obligations as anyone else in business. The state and federal government will want to know and get a report of exactly what sales you made on your book so, keep good records. I utilize all methods of keeping track of receipts and spending toward the production, printing, publishing and profit of my books and you should too.

Do your homework, ask questions, seek legal advice and make sure that your personal assets and family are protected throughout this process.

Some global distribution companies require tax information before they will establish your account and allow you to upload your book and receive payments. If you do not have this process taken care of then your book sales could be held up until the financial legalities are worked out.

No matter how you decide to sell your book, whether it be on your website, at live events, or out of the back of your car, it is important to know that people will not only pay with cash but with credit card so, make sure that you have a way to receive these payments. Don't lose out on a sale because you don't take credit cards. Check out www.paypal.com, www.squareup.com or your local bank for merchant information and processes to receive payments.

Printing

Once your book is edited, formatted and the book cover is done then it will be time to find a printer and distributor for your book.

Decide if you want your book to be paperback, hardback or an eBook. I suggest that your book be available in all formats. Don't miss out on a customer or sale because your book is not in the format that they like.

I publish all of my personal books in all formats for multiple sales outlets and customer preferences. I am always looking for more ways to sell books that are mine and my client's. Each format has a different set-up but with a final draft of a book book, the adjustment in formatting can be made easily to accommodate the specifications.

The cheapest and easiest printer and distributor for paperback books is www.Createspace.com. They are owned and operated by Amazon, which is the largest online distributor to date. With Createspace, you are guided through the process of formatting and uploading your book's cover and interior in paperback format. They do not print in hardbound format. For a fee, they will also provide you with experts to help with the process. It is not cheap but if you need help then they will be there for you and if you need our help then we can assist you as well. Reach out to us at www.bkroystonpublishing.com or email us at bkroystonpublishing@gmail.com.

There are several printers and distributors that are out there to assist you with getting your book out into the world. Below is a very short list of printers and distribution outlets. Check them out by asking questions, and connecting with other authors who have used their services.

48 Hour Books – Printing only! No distribution.

Ingram

Baker and Taylor

Lightning Source

Ingram Spark

NOOK Press

KINDLE

_____

_____

_____

_____

_____

_____

_____

_____

_____

_____

_____

_____

_____

_____

_____

_____

_____

_____

_____

Proof Copy of the Book

Once you have selected a printer then you are ready to upload your book and receive a proof copy. I request a proof copy of each and every book that I publish. At times, I have requested and purchased multiple proof copies to make sure that the book was right.

The proof copy is the first copy of the finished version of your book. The proof copy shows you how the book will look after it is printed.

Go through the proof copy page by page, and line by line. The computer screen will not do the final printed proof copy justice because things shift or are adjusted in the printing process. When the book is uploaded and formatted for printing, some of the words may move or some of the cover may be cut off because it doesn't meet specifications. There are some printers who won't even print the book for a proof copy because it doesn't meet the specifications. Make the adjustments so that your book's proof copy won't be delayed.

Once you have received your proof copy, mark or get a stack of post-it notes to flag any and all of the mistakes, formatting errors or book cover errors that you see throughout the proof copy. My proof copies are always marked up with pen and post-its.

Some things you won't catch going through the book yourself so, give the proof copy to a friend. Pay them with a gift card or take them to dinner but you need a second set of eyes to look at the book for errors. Remember that you know what you wanted to say but somehow it may have been missed or overlooked.

You want your book to be as close to perfect as humanly possible so, order a proof copy of your book. You won't regret it.

Each printing and distribution outlet should have helpful technical support to assist you in the process of uploading and printing your book.

Make sure that you check all of the information on their website before setting up an account or making a payment. If you get stuck or need help then just reach out to them and don't forget to check out the video series that goes along with this book. If you need any more help from us in any part of the publishing process then reach out to us at www.bkroystonpublishing.com or email us at bkroystonpublishing@gmail.com or call 502-802-5385.

Get the Entire Write. Publish. Promote
Series Today by visiting:
http://www.Writepublishpromoteitnowno
w.com

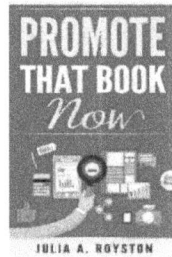

About the Author

Julia Royston is an author, publisher and motivational speaker born and raised in Louisville, KY. Julia is the oldest of three daughters born to a Christian family and she is married to Mr. Brian K. Royston. Julia has a Bachelors in Accounting, a Masters in information science and a doctorate in Religious Education. She is a public elementary school Computer Technology Teacher and Media Specialist.

Julia has appeared on The Bobby Jones Presents New Artist Showcase and ministered with notables such as Dr. Jackie McCullough, Pastor Donnie McClurkin, Bishop Noel Jones, Bishop Tudor Bismarck, Myron Williams and Bishop Richard "Mr. Clean" White. In December 2004 and 2005, Julia toured Switzerland with the Voices of Gospel Concert Series.

Julia has been singing since she was nine years old and to date has recorded several musical projects including, "Joy in His

Presence", "A New Season in Word and Song", "Hymns for Him", "For Your Glory Lord" and in the Fall of 2016 is set to release her next full project, "Begin Again."

In 2002, Julia established 'For the Kingdom Ministries' with the mission to "Build God's People to Build the Kingdom of God" through education, empowerment and encouragement through inspirational music, high quality materials and messages of hope.

In 2011, BK Royston Publishing Company was established and released its first book titled, "How Hot is Your Love Life? Return to Your first Love." To date Julia Royston has published twenty of her own books with BK Royston Publishing Company, LLC. She has signed thirty authors to her company and published more than sixty books. For more information about BK Royston Publishing, click here and visithttp://bkroystonpublishing.com.

Julia Royston Enterprises LLC was established in 2013 to assist people to walk in their purpose through transformational virtual, group and individual coaching. Visit: http://www.juliaroystonenterprises.com to learn more about and sign up for the many coaching programs offered by Julia Royston Enterprises.

In 2015, a second publishing company, Royal Media Publishing was established to provide an outlet for authors with mainstream topics as well as bring forth a global audience.

Currently, Julia Royston hosts a daily motivational Periscope called Julia Royston, the "Message Motivator", and "When Authors Meet" which provide workshops for authors around the country as well as authors who are at retreats, and conferences. These workshops also appeal to masterminds of business.

The year 2016 marks the five year anniversary of BK Royston Publishing and Julia continues to travel the country speaking, singing, empowering and inspiring people. She hopes to inspire those whom she encounters to write and publish their books as well as to live the abundant life that is their Purpose and Destiny.

Keep up with Julia on Social Media by following or liking her pages on Facebook, Twitter, LinkedIn, Instagram, Youtube Channel and Periscope.

www.ingramcontent.com/pod-product-compliance
Lightning Source LLC
Chambersburg PA
CBHW072212270326
41930CB00011B/2616